CHRIST'S SYMPATHY TO WEARY PILGRIMS

by Octavius Winslow

(1808 - 1878)

WHAT A BOUNDLESS, FATHOMLESS OCEAN!

Eternal love moved the heart of Jesus to relinquish heaven for earth—a diadem for a cross—the robe of divine majesty for the garment of our nature; by taking upon Himself the leprosy of our sin. Oh, the infinite love of Christ! What a boundless, fathomless ocean! Ask the ransomed of the Lord, whose chains He has dissolved, whose dungeon He has opened, whose liberty He has conferred, if there ever was love like His!

What shall we say of the ransom price? It was the richest, the costliest, that Heaven could give. He gave Himself for us! What more could He do? He gave Himself; body, soul and spirit. He gave His time, His labor, His blood, His life, His ALL, as the price for our ransom, the cost of our redemption. He carried the wood and reared the altar. Then, bearing His bosom to the stroke of the uplifted and descending arm of the Father, paid the price of our salvation in the warm lifeblood of His heart!

What a boundless, fathomless ocean! How is it that we feel the force and exemplify the practical influence of this amazing, all commanding truth so faintly? Oh, the desperate depravity of our nature! Oh, the deep iniquity of our iniquitous hearts! Will not the blood drops of Jesus move us? Will not the agonies of the cross influence us? Will not His dying love constrain us to a more heavenly life?

LEAN HARD!

"Cast your burden upon the Lord, and he shall sustain you." Psalm 55:22

It is by an act of simple, prayerful faith we transfer our cares and anxieties, our sorrows and needs, to the Lord. Jesus invites you come and lean upon Him, and to lean with all your might upon that arm that balances the universe, and upon that bosom that bled for you upon the soldier's spear! But you doubtingly ask, "Is the Lord able to do this thing for me ?" And thus, while you are debating a matter about which there is not the shadow of a shade of doubt, the burden is crushing your gentle spirit to the dust. And all the while Jesus stands at your side and lovingly says, "Cast your burden upon Me and I will sustain you. I am God Almighty. I bore the load of your sin and condemnation up the steep of Calvary, and the same power of omnipotence, and the same strength of love that bore it all for you then, is prepared to bear your need and sorrow now. Roll it all upon Me! Child of My love! Lean hard! Let Me feel the pressure of your care. I know your burden, child! I shaped it—I poised it in My own hand and made no proportion of its weight to your unaided strength. For even as I laid it on, I said I shall be near, and while she leans on Me, this burden shall be Mine, not hers. So shall I keep My child within the encircling arms of My own love. Here lay it down! Do not fear to impose it on a shoulder which upholds the government of worlds! Yet closer come! You are not near enough! I would embrace your burden, so I might feel My child reposing on My breast. You love Me! I know it. Doubt not, then. But, loving me, lean hard!"

THE FLAMING SWORD OF JUSTICE QUENCHED IN THE HOLY, LOVING BOSOM OF JESUS!

The most significant and appalling demonstration of God's holiness that the universe ever beheld, infinitely distancing and transcending every other, is the sufferings and death of His only and beloved Son! The cross of Calvary exhibits God's hatred and punishment of sin in a way and to an extent which the annihilation of millions of worlds, swept from the face of the universe by the broom of His wrath, could never have done! "Who his own self bare our sins in his own body on the tree."

Behold the most awful display of God's hatred of sin! Finding the sins of the Church upon Christ as its Surety, Substitute, and Savior, the wrath of God was poured out upon Him without measure! God finding the sins of His people laid upon His Son, emptied upon His holy soul all the vials of His wrath due to their transgressions! Go, my soul, to Calvary, and learn how holy God is, and what a monstrous thing sin is, and how imperiously, solemnly, and holily bound Jehovah is to punish it, either in the person of the sinner, or in the person of a Surety. Never was the Son of God dearer to the Father than at the very moment that the sword of divine justice, flaming and flashing, pierced to its hilt His holy heart!

But it was the wrath of God, not against His beloved Son, but against the sins which met on Him when presenting Himself on the cross as the substitutionary sacrifice and offering for His Church—He gave Himself for us. What a new conception must angels have formed of the exceeding sinfulness of sin, when they beheld the flaming sword of justice quenched in the holy, loving bosom of Jesus! And in what a dazzling light does this fact place the marvelous love of God to sinners! Man's sin and God's love; the indescribable enormity of the one, and the immeasurable greatness of the other; are exhibited in the cross of Christ as nowhere else. Oh, to learn experimentally these two great facts—sin's infinite hatefulness, and love's infinite holiness! The love of God in giving His Son to die; the love of Christ in dying; the essential turpitude and unmitigated enormity of sin, which demanded a sacrifice so Divine, so holy, and so precious!

SO FATHOMLESS, BOUNDLESS, AND INEXHAUSTIBLE!

Christ is wonderful in His love. Love was the first and eternal link in the golden chain lowered from the highest throne in heaven down to the lowest depth of earth. That Christ should love us was the beginning of wonders. When we endeavor to comprehend that love, measure it, fathom it, scale it—we learn that it has heights we cannot reach, depths we cannot sound, lengths and breadths we cannot measure! Such love, such divine love, such infinite love, such everlasting love, such redeeming, dying love, is an ocean whose eternal waves waft into our fallen world every wonder of God and of heaven.

That Jesus should love such beings as us—that He should love us while we were yet sinners—that He should set His heart upon us, choose us, die for us, call us, and finally bring us to glory, knowing what we were, and what we would prove to be—oh, this is wondrous love indeed! Plunge into this fathomless, boundless Ocean of love, O sin-burdened one! It will cover all your sins, it will efface all your guilt; it will flood over all your unworthiness— and, floating upon its golden waves, it will gently waft you to the shore of eternal blessedness!

How often have you wondered why Christ should set His heart upon such a one as you! And is it not a wonder that, amid all your fickleness and backslidings and cold, base returns, this love of God towards you has not chilled or changed? But do not rest, do not be satisfied with your present limited experience of Christ's wonderful love. It is so marvelously great. This Ocean of love is so fathomless, boundless, and inexhaustible, you may plunge, with all your infirmities, sins, and sorrows, into its fullness, exclaiming, "O, the depth!" The well is deep! Drink abundantly, O beloved!

LOVE SUFFERING, AND BLEEDING, AND EXPIRING!

The love of Christ! Such a precious theme! Of it can we ever weary? Never! Its greatness can we ever know? Never! Its plenitude can we fully contain? Never! Its depths cannot be fathomed, its dimensions cannot be measured! It passes knowledge! All that Jesus did for His people was but the unfolding and expression of His love.

Traveling to Bethlehem—I see love incarnate! Tracking His steps as He went about doing good—I see love laboring! Visiting the house of Bethany—I see love sympathizing! Standing by the grave of Lazarus—I see love weeping! Entering the gloomy precincts of Gethsemane—I see love sorrowing! Passing on to Calvary—I see love suffering, and bleeding, and expiring! The whole scene of His life is but an unfolding of the deep, and awesome, and precious mystery of redeeming love!

IT IS I

"Be of good cheer: it is I; be not afraid." Mark 6:50

Listen, then, to the voice of Jesus in the storm. It is I who raised the tempest in your soul, and will control it. It is I who sent your affliction, and will be with you in it. It is I who kindled the furnace, and will watch the flames, and bring you through it. It is I who formed your burden, who carved your cross, and who will strengthen you to bear it. It is I who mixed your cup of grief, and will enable you to drink it with meek submission to your Father's will. It is I who took from you worldly substance, who bereft you of your child, of the wife of your bosom, of the husband of your youth, and will be infinitely better to you than husband, wife, or child. It is I who have done it ALL.

I make the clouds my chariot, and clothe myself with the tempest as with a garment. The night hour is my time of coming, and the dark, surging waves are the pavement upon which I walk. Take courage! It is I. Don't be afraid. It is I—your Friend, your Brother, your Savior! I am causing all the circumstances of your life to work together for your good. It is I who permitted the enemy to assail you, the slander to blast you, the unkindness to wound you, the need to press you! Your affliction did not spring out of the ground, but came down from above—a heaven sent blessing disguised as an angel of light clad in a robe of ebony.

I have sent all in love! This sickness is not unto death, but for the glory of God. This bereavement shall not always bow you to the earth, nor drape in changeless gloom your life. It is I who ordered, arranged, and controlled it all! In every stormy wind, in every darksome night, in every lonesome hour, in every rising fear, the voice of Jesus shall be heard, saying, "Be of good cheer: it is I; be not afraid."

THE PERSONAL ATTRACTIONS OF JESUS!

The love of Jesus wins us. His glory charms us. His beauty attracts us. His sympathy soothes us. His gentleness subdues us. His faithfulness inspires us. He is the altogether lovely One! Jesus is all that is tender in love. Jesus is all that is wise in counsel. Jesus is all that is patient and kind. Jesus is all that is faithful in friendship. Jesus is all that is balmy, soothing, and healing. The heart of Jesus is ever loving towards His children. The disposition of Jesus is ever kind towards His children. The nature of Jesus is ever sympathizing towards His children.

Jesus is your Brother, your Friend, your Redeemer. As your Brother, He knows the needs of His brethren in adversity. As your Friend, He shows Himself friendly. As your Redeemer, He has redeemed your soul from sin and hell. Jesus has ascended up on high to take possession of heaven on your behalf, and to prepare a place for you! Upon His heart He wears your name as a precious pearl in the priestly breastplate. There is not a moment of your time, nor an event of your life, nor a circumstance of your daily history, nor a mental or spiritual emotion of yours, in which you are not borne upon the love, and remembered in the ceaseless intercession of Christ. The personal attractions of Jesus are all-inviting and irresistible!

A FATHER'S HAND!

"My times are in your hand." Psalm 31:15

Our times of adversity are also in God's hand. As every sunbeam that brightens, so every cloud that darkens, comes from God. We are subject to great and sudden reverses in our earthly condition. Joy is often succeeded by grief, prosperity by adversity. We are on the pinnacle today, tomorrow at its bottom. Oh! What a change may one event and one moment create! But, beloved, ALL is from the Lord.

Afflictions do not spring from the soil, nor does trouble sprout from the ground. Sorrow cannot come until God bids it. Until God in His sovereignty permits—health cannot fade, wealth cannot vanish, comfort cannot decay, friendship cannot chill, and loved ones cannot die. Your time of sorrow is His appointment. The bitter cup which it may please the Lord that you shall drink this year will not be mixed by human hands. In the hand of the Lord is that cup! Some treasure you are now pressing to your heart, He may ask you to resign. Some blessing you now possess, He may bid you to relinquish. Some fond expectation you now cherish, He may will that you should forego. Some lonely path, He may design that you should tread.

Yes, He may even bereave you of all, and yet all, ALL is in His hand! His hand! A Father's hand, moving in thick darkness, is shaping every event, and arranging every detail in your life! Has sickness laid you on a bed of suffering? Has bereavement darkened your home? Has adversity impoverished your resources? Has change lessened your comforts? Has sorrow in one of its many forms crushed your spirit to the earth? The Lord has done it! In all that has been sent, in all that has be recalled, and in all that has been withheld—His hand, noiseless and unseen has brought it about!

Ah! yes, that hand of changeless love blends a sweet with every bitter—pencils a bright rainbow in each dark cloud—upholds each faltering step—shelters within its hollow—and guides with unerring skill, His chosen people safe to eternal glory! Dear child of God, your afflictions, your trials, your crosses, your losses, your sorrows, all, ALL are in your heavenly Father's hand, and they cannot come until sent by Him!

Bow that stricken heart—yield that tempest-tossed soul to His sovereign disposal, to His calm, righteous sway, in the submissive spirit and language of your suffering Savior, "May Your will, O my Father! not mine, be done. My times of sadness and of grief are in Your hand." Beloved, all is in your Father's hand! Be those times what they may—times of trial, times of temptation, times of suffering, times of peril, times of sunshine or of gloom, or times of life or death, they are in your Father's hand!

Has the Lord seen fit to recall some fond blessing, to deny some earnest request, or painfully to discipline your heart? All this springs from a Father's love as fully as though He had unlocked His treasury and poured its costliest gifts at your feet! All of our times are in our Redeemer's hands! That same Redeemer who carried our sorrows in His heart, our curse and sins on His soul, our cross on His shoulder; who died, who rose again, and who lives and intercedes for us, and who will gather all His ransomed around Him in glory, is your Guardian and your

Guide! Your times are in the hands of Him who still bears the print of the nails!

FOR YOU!

Is Jesus precious to your heart? Is He the object of your supreme admiration and delight? Does He have your warmest affection? Do you love Jesus? You must light your torch of affection for Christ, at the altar of Calvary. You must go there, and learn and believe what the love of Jesus is to you—the vastness of that love; the self sacrifice of that love; how that love of Christ labored and wept, bled, suffered, and died for you! Can you stand before this love; this love so precious, so great, so enduring, so self-consuming, so changeless; and know that for you was this offering—for you this cross—for you this agony—for you this scorn and insult—for you this death; and feel no sensibility, no emotion, no love to Jesus? Impossible!

Do not be cast down, then, in vain regrets that your love to Christ is so frigid, so fickle, so dubious. Go and muse upon the reality and the greatness of the Savior's love to you, and if love can inspire love, while you muse, the fire will burn, and your soul shall be all in flame with love to God!

LIFE IS LIKE A PAINTED DREAM

"For this God is our God for ever and ever: he will be our guide even unto death." Psalm 48:14

The world passes away. Everything here in this present world is changing.

"Life is like a painted dream;

Like the rapid summer stream;

Like the fleeting meteor's ray;

Like the shortest winter's day;

Like the fitful breeze that sighs;

Like the waning flame that dies;

Darting, dazzling on the eye;

Fading in eternity."

A rope of sand, a spider's web, a silken thread, a passing shadow, an ebbing wave, are the most fitting and expressive emblems of all things belonging to this present earthly state. The homes that sheltered us in childhood we leave. The land which gave us birth we leave. The loved ones who encircled our hearths pass away. The friends of early years depart. And the world that was so sunny, and life that was so sweet, is all beclouded and embittered—the whole scenery of existence changed into wintry gloom. Such are the saddening, depressing effects of life's vicissitudes.

But in the midst of all, "this God is our God for ever and ever!" All beings change but God. All things change but heaven. The evolutions of time revolve, the events of earth go onward, but He upon whom all things hang, and by whom all events are shaped and controlled, moves not. "For I am the Lord, I change not." Our affairs may alter. Our circumstances may change. Our relations and friends may depart one by one. Our souls in a single day pass through many fluctuations of spiritual feeling. But He who chose us to be His own, and who has kept us to the present moment, is our covenant God and Father forever and ever, and will never throw us off and cast us away. "For this God is our God for ever and ever: he will be our guide even unto death."

FOR ME, A WORM!

O what a truth is this! The Son of God offering Himself up a sacrifice for sin! He who knew no sin—who was holy, harmless, and undefiled—not one thought of evil in His heart, yet made sin, or a sin offering! O the magnitude of the thought! If God Himself had not declared it, we could not have believed it, though an angel's trumpet had announced it.

O blessed and adorable Immanuel! Was this the end and design of Your intense and mysterious sufferings? Was it that You should obey, bear the sin, endure the curse, and bow Your head in death, that I might go free? Was it in my stead, and in my behalf? O unexampled love! O infinite and free grace! That God should become incarnate—that the Holy One should so take upon Him sin, as to be dealt with by stern justice as though He were Himself the sinner—that He should drain the cup of wrath, give His back to the smiters, endure the shame and the spitting, and at last be suspended upon the cross, and pour out His last drop of most precious blood—and all this for me! For me a rebel! For me a worm! For me the chief of sinners! Be astonished, O heavens! and be amazed, O earth! Was ever love like this?

THE TEARS OF JESUS!

"Jesus wept." John 11:35

These are among the most wonderful words recorded in the Bible. They mark the most exquisitely tender, touching, and expressive incident in His whole life. "Jesus wept"—wept from emotion, wept from sympathy. Is there a more consolatory, soothing view of Christ's love than this? It is a compassionate, sympathizing, weeping love!

The sympathy of Jesus never wearies or slumbers, it never chills or forgets. It entwines with our every cross— attaches to our every burden—and frosts with sparkling light, each darkling cloud. It is not the vapid sentiment of fiction, nor the morbid sympathy of romance. It is a divine-human reality. It is the sympathetic love of the Incarnate God!

Let your faith, then, repose with confidence on the reality of Christ's sympathy with your grief. Oh how sacred and precious are the tears of divine love—the tears of Jesus! Soothed and sustained by such a sympathy as Christ's, we may well drink meekly the cup our Father mingles—we can well afford to be severed from all other sympathy, and weep out our sorrow in lonely places—Jesus sympathizing with us by the couch of languor, by the bed of darkness, and at the grave of buried love.

O afflicted one, tossed with tempest and not comforted, refuse not this cup of consolation which the Holy Spirit, the Comforter, would give you—the sympathy of your Lord and Savior, your Friend and Brother in the time of your calamity. Yield yourself to its irresistible power, and it will draw you submissively to His feet, and hush to rest your sobbing heart upon His bosom!

WHY THEN, THESE FEARS? WHY THIS DISTRUST?

Jesus has all the treasures of the everlasting covenant, all the fullness of the Godhead, all the resources of the universe in His keeping, and at His disposal! Look at the starry sky—Jesus strewed it with its jewelry. Look at that enchanting landscape—Jesus enameled it with its loveliness. Look at that cloud-capped mountain—Jesus reared it. Look at that beauteous lily—Jesus painted it. Look at that soaring bird—Jesus feeds it.

He, with whom is all this strength and beauty, is your Brother! Are you not better and dearer to Him than these? He has loved and chosen you from all eternity, ransomed you with His blood, and inhabited you by His Spirit. Why, then, these fears? Why this distrust? All He requires of you is to bring to His fullness your emptiness—to His sympathy your grief—to His unerring wisdom your confusion—and to His sheltering wing your temptations and trials. Spread your case before Him in the humble confidence of a child. Listen to His words—"I am the Lord your God, which brought you out of the land of Egypt: open your mouth wide, and I will fill it."

CHRIST'S SLEEPLESS VIGILANCE OVER HIS PEOPLE!

What an exalted and endearing truth is Christ's sleepless vigilance over his people! Imagine yourself threading your way along a most difficult and perilous path, every step of which is attended with pain and jeopardy, and is taken with hesitancy and doubt. Unknown to you and unseen, there is One hovering around you each moment—checking each false step—and guiding each doubtful one—soothing each sorrow—and supplying each need. All is calm and silent. Not a sound is heard, not a movement is seen; and yet, to your amazement, just at the critical moment, the needed support comes—you know not from where, you know not from whom. This is no picture of imagination.

Are you a child of God on your pilgrimage to paradise by an intricate and a perilous way? Jesus is near to you at each moment, unseen and often unknown. You have at times stood speechless with awe at the strange interposition on your behalf, of providence and of grace—no visible sign indicated the source of your help. There was no echo of footfall at your side, no flitting of shadow athwart your path. No law of nature was altered nor suspended, the sun did not stand still, nor did the heavens open. And yet deliverance, strange and effectual deliverance, came at a moment most unexpected, yet most needed.

It was Jesus your Redeemer, your Brother, your Shepherd, and your Guide! He it was who, hovering around you—unknown and unobserved, kept you as the apple of His eye, and sheltered you in the hollow of His hand. It was He who armed you with bravery for the fight—who poured strength into your spirit—and grace into your heart, when the full weight of calamity pressed upon them. Thus has He always been to His children. The eye that neither slumbers nor sleeps was upon you! He knew in what furnace you were placed, and was there to temper the flame when it seemed the severest. He saw your frail vessel struggling through the tempest, and He came to your rescue at the height of the storm!

How has He proved this in seasons of difficulty and doubt! How often, at a crisis the most critical of your history, the Lord has appeared for you! Your lack has been supplied—your doubt has been solved—and your perplexity has been guided. He has delivered your soul from death—your eyes from tears—and your feet from falling. You are never for an instant out of His heart—out of His thoughts—out of His hands—or out of His eye! Go then, and lay your weariness on Christ.

Take your bereaved, stricken and bleeding heart to Him!

What is your sorrow? Has the hand of death smitten? Is the beloved one removed? Has the desire of your eyes been taken away with a stroke? But who has done it? Jesus has done it! Death was only His messenger. Your Jesus has done it. The Lord has taken away. And what has He removed? Your wife? Ah, Jesus has all the tenderness that your wife ever had. Hers was only a drop from the ocean that is in His heart. Is it your husband? Jesus is better to you than ten husbands. Is it your parent, your child, your friend, your all of earthly bliss? Is the cistern broken? Is the earthen vessel dashed to pieces? Are all your streams dry? Jesus is still enough. He has not taken Himself from you, and never, never will.

Take your bereaved, stricken and bleeding heart to Him—and rest it upon His heart, which was once bereaved, stricken and bleeding, too! He knows how to bind up the broken heart, to heal the wounded spirit and to comfort those who mourn.

What is your sorrow? Has health failed you? Has property forsaken you? Have friends turned against you? Are you tried in your circumstances? Perplexed in your path? Are providences thickening and darkening around you? Are you anticipating seasons of approaching trial? Are you walking in darkness, having no light? Simply go to Jesus! He is an ever open door—a tender, loving, faithful Friend, ever near. He is a Brother born for your adversity. His grace and sympathy are sufficient for you. Go to Him in every trial—cast upon Him every burden—take the infirmity, the corruption, the cross as it arises—simply and immediately to Jesus! Jesus is your loving and confiding Brother and Friend, to go to at all times and under all circumstances.

LOOKING AT THE WORLD THROUGH THE CROSS

Jesus could accomplish man's redemption in no other way than by crucifixion—He must die, and die the death of the cross. What light and glory beam around the cross! Of what prodigies of grace is it the instrument, of what glorious truths is it the symbol, of what mighty, magic power is it the source! Around it gathers all the light of the Old Testament economy. It explains every symbol—it substantiates every shadow—it solves every mystery—it fulfills every type—it confirms every prophecy of that dispensation which had eternally remained unmeaning and inexplicable except for the death of the Son of God upon the cross.

Not the past only, but all future splendor gathers around the cross of our Lord Jesus Christ. It assures us of the ultimate reign of the Savior and tells of the reward which shall spring from His sufferings—and while its one arm points to the divine counsels of eternity past, with the other it points to the future triumph and glory of Christ's kingdom in the eternity to come. Such is the lowly yet sublime—the weak yet mighty instrument by which the sinner is saved and God eternally glorified.

The cross of Christ was in Paul's view the grand consummation of all preceding dispensations of God to men. The cross of Christ was the meritorious procuring cause of all spiritual blessings to our fallen race. The cross of Christ was the scene of Christ's splendid victories over all His enemies and ours. The cross of Christ was the most powerful incentive to all evangelical holiness. The cross of Christ was the instrument which was to subjugate the world to the supremacy of Jesus. The cross of Christ was the source of all true peace, joy, and hope. The cross of Christ is the tree beneath whose shadow all sin expired, all grace lived.

The cross of our Lord Jesus Christ! What a holy thrill these words produce in the heart of those who love the Savior! How significant their meaning—how precious their influence! Marvelous and irresistible is the power of the cross! The cross of Christ has subdued many a rebellious will. The cross of Christ has broken many a marble heart. The cross of Christ has laid low many a vaunting foe. The cross of Christ has overcome and triumphed when all other instruments have failed. The cross of Christ has transformed the lion-like heart of man, into the lamb-like heart of Christ. And when lifted up in its own naked simplicity and inimitable grandeur, the cross of Christ has won and attracted millions to its faith, admiration, and love!

What a marvelous power does this cross of Jesus possess! It changes the Christian's entire judgment of the world. Looking at the world through the cross, his opinion is totally revolutionized. He sees it as it really is—a sinful, empty, vain thing. He learns its iniquity, in that it crucified the Lord of life and glory. His expectations from the world, his love to the world, are changed. He has found another object of love—the Savior whom the world cast out and slew. And his love to the world is destroyed by that power which alone could destroy it—the crucifying power of the cross.

It is the cross which eclipses, in the view of the true believer, the glory and attraction of every other object. What is the weapon by which faith combats with and overcomes the world? What but the cross of Jesus! Just as the natural eye, gazing for a while upon the sun, is blinded for the moment, by its overpowering effulgence, to all other objects—so to the believer, concentrating his mind upon the glory of the crucified Savior, studying closely the wonders of grace and love and truth meeting in the cross—the world with all its attraction fades into the full darkness of an eclipse. Are not Christ and His cross infinitely better than the world and its love? "But God forbid that I should glory, save in the cross of our Lord Jesus Christ, by whom the world is crucified unto me, and I unto the world."

BRING YOUR SORROWS TO ME

"Bring him here to me." Matthew 17:17

In your moment of disappointment and despair, Jesus meets you with the gracious words, "Bring it here unto me." And now your spirit revives, your heart bounds, at the words, and you exclaim, "Behold, Lord, I come."

Jesus says, "Bring your sorrows to Me." Never did the soul find so powerful a magnet, attracting to itself affliction in every form, and sorrow in every shade, as Jesus. Standing as in the center of a world of woe, He invites every daughter of sorrow, of sin, of grief to repair to Him for support, sympathy, and healing. As the High Priest of His Church for whom alone He suffered, and wept, and sobbed, He unveils a bosom capacious enough and loving enough, and sympathizing enough, to embrace every sufferer, and to pillow every grief. Accept, then, His compassionate invitation, and bring your grief to the soothing, sustaining, sanctifying grace of His heart!

THIS DIVINE SECRET!

"Casting all your care upon him; for he cares for you."
1 Peter 5:7

How full of soothing and repose are these words! Where, in the world's wilderness, grows the flower of heart's-ease as it blooms and blossoms here? What cares have they lightened! What anxieties have they removed! What burdens have they unclasped! What springs of joy and comfort and hope have they unsealed in many a sad and oppressed heart! But do you not, beloved reader, need to be put in constant remembrance of this divine secret—of rest amid toil—of repose amid disquietude—of soothing amid corroding cares—and of confidence and hope in the midst of change and depression?

Bewildered and oppressed by the multitude of anxious thoughts within you—is there not a danger of being so absorbed by the care as to overlook the Caretaker? to forget the heart's ease in the overwhelming of the heart's anxiety? Cast all your anxiety on Him because He cares for you!

FOR ME, A POOR, WORTHLESS SINNER!

"Who his own self bare our sins in his own body on the tree, that we, being dead to sins, should live unto righteousness: by whose stripes ye were healed." 1 Peter 2:24

Blessed announcement! Not the less hateful, nor hated, is the sin because it is forgiven and entirely blotted out. Oh no! Let the Lord touch your heart, Christian reader, with a sense of His pardoning love, with the assurance of His forgiveness—and you will go and hate, and mortify, and forsake it, more resolutely and effectually than ever! And must the Son of God become the Son of man, that those who are by nature children of wrath, might become the sons of God! Must God, the eternal God, the high and lofty One, stoop so low as to become incarnate, and that for sinners—for me, a poor worthless sinner!

To save me from eternal woe, must Jesus suffer, agonize, and die—die in my stead, die for my sins, die an accursed death! Ah! Lord, what must sin be—what must my sin be! How little have I thought of it, how little have I mourned for it, still less have I hated it as I ought to have hated it! Lord, how vile, how unutterably vile I am! Oh hated sin! Do You forgive it, Father of my mercies? This only makes it more hateful still.

THE WRATH OF GOD LET LOOSE UPON HIS SON!

Divine holiness is best exhibited in the cross of Jesus. Not hell itself, dreadful and eternal as is its suffering—the undying worm, the unquenchable fire, the smoke of the torment that goes up forever and ever—affords such a solemn and impressive spectacle of the holiness and justice of God in the punishment of sin, as is presented in the death of God's beloved Son.

An eminent Puritan writer thus strikingly puts it— "Not all the vials of judgment that have or shall be poured out upon this wicked world—nor the flaming furnace of a sinner's conscience—nor the irrevocable sentence pronounced against the rebellious devils—nor the groans of the damned creatures—give such a demonstration of God's hatred of sin, as the wrath of God let loose upon His Son!"

Never did Divine holiness appear more beautiful and lovely than at the time our Savior's countenance was most marred in the midst of His dying groans. This He Himself acknowledges in that penitential psalm, when God turned His smiling face away from Him, and thrust His sharp knife into His heart, which forced that terrible cry from Him, "My God, my God, why hast thou forsaken me? why art thou so far from helping me, and from the words of my roaring? But thou art holy."

Such an impressive view of God's holiness the angels in heaven never before beheld—not even when they saw the non-elect spirits hurled from the heights of glory down to the bottomless pit, to be reserved in chains of darkness and woe forever! Jesus was the innocent One dying for the guilty ones—the holy One dying for the sinful ones!

Divine justice, in its mission of judgment, as it swept by the cross, found the Son of God impaled upon its wood beneath the sins and the curse of His people. Upon Him its judgment fell—on His soul its wrath was poured—in His heart its flaming sword was plunged—and thus, from Him, justice exacted the full penalty of man's transgression—the last farthing of the great debt!

Go to the cross, then, my reader, and learn the holiness of God. Contemplate the dignity of Christ—His preciousness to His Father's heart—the sinlessness of His nature. And then behold—the sorrow of His soul—the torture of His body—the tragedy of His death—the abasement—the ignominy—the humiliation—into the fathomless depths of which the whole transaction plunged our incarnate God! And let me ask, standing, as you are, before this unparalleled spectacle, "Can you cherish low views of God's holiness, or light views of your own sinfulness?"

OH, ENCOURAGING TRUTH!

"I the Lord search the heart." Jeremiah 17:10

Solemn as is this view of the Divine character, the believing mind finds in it sweet and hallowed repose. What more consolatory truth in some of the most trying positions of a child of God than this—the Lord knows the heart! The world condemns us, and the saints may wrongly judge us—but God knows the heart! And to those who have been led into deep discoveries of their heart's hidden evil, to whom have been made startling and distressing unveilings, how precious is this character of God, "I the Lord search the heart."

Is there a single recess of our hearts we would veil from His penetrating glance? Is there a corruption we would hide from His view? Is there an evil of which we would have Him ignorant? Oh no! Mournful and humiliating as is the spectacle, we would throw open every door, and uplift every window, and invite and urge His scrutiny and inspection, making no concealments, and indulging in no reserves, and framing no excuses when dealing with the great Searcher of hearts, exclaiming, "Search me, O God, and know my heart: try me, and know my thoughts: And see if there be any wicked way in me, and lead me in the way everlasting."

And while the Lord is thus acquainted with the evil of our hearts, He most graciously conceals that evil from the eyes of others. He seems to say, by His benevolent conduct, "I see my child's infirmity." Then, covering it with His hand, exclaims, "but no other eye shall see it, but my own!" Oh, the touching tenderness, the loving kindness of our

God! Knowing, as He does, all the evil of our nature, He yet veils that evil from human eye—that others may not despise us as we often despise ourselves. Who but God could know it? Who but God would conceal it?

And how blessed, too, to remember that while God knows all the evil, He is as intimately acquainted with all the good that is in the hearts of His people! He knows all that His Spirit has implanted—all that His grace has wrought. Oh encouraging truth! That spark of love, faint and flickering—that pulsation of life, low and tremulous—that touch of faith, feeble and hesitating—that groan, that sigh—that low thought of self that leads a man to seek the shade—that self-abasement that places his mouth in the dust—oh, not one of these sacred emotions is unseen, unnoticed by God! His eye ever rests with infinite compassion and delight on His own image in the renewed soul.

YOUR PRESENT ADVERSITY

"And we know that all things work together for good
to those who love God, to those who are the called
according to his purpose." Romans 8:28

It is palpably clear and emphatically true that all that
occurs in the Lord's government of His people conspires
for, and works out, and results in, their highest happiness
and their greatest good. The gloomiest and most painful
circumstances in the history of the child of God, without a
solitary exception, are all conspiring, and all working
together, for his real and permanent good.

The painful and inexplicable dispensations, which at
the present moment may be thickening and deepening
around your path, are but so many mysteries in God's
government, which He is working out to their certain,
satisfactory, and happy results. And when the good thus
embosomed in the lowering cloud of some crushing
providence, accomplishes its benevolent and heaven-sent
mission, then trial will expand its dark pinions and fly
away—and sorrow will roll up its somber drapery and
disappear!

All things under the government of an infinitely great,
all-wise, righteous, and beneficent Lord God, work
together for good. What that good may be—the shape it
may assume—the complexion it may wear—the end to
which it may be subservient—we cannot tell. To our dim
view it may appear an evil, but to God's far seeing eye it is
a positive good. Oh, truth most divine! Oh, words most
consolatory!

How many whose eye traces this page, it may be whose tears bedew it, whose sighs breathe over it, whose prayers hallow it, may be wading in deep waters, may be drinking bitter cups, and are ready to exclaim—"All these things are against me!" Oh no, beloved of God, all these things are for you! Do not be afraid! Christ restrains the flood upon whose heaving bosom He serenely sits. Christ controls the waters, whose sounding waves obey the mandate of His voice. Christ's cloudy chariot is paved with love! Then, fear not! Your Father grasps the helm of your storm-tossed vessel—and through cloud and tempest will steer it safely to the port of endless rest!

Will it not be a real good, if your present adversity results in the dethronement of some worshiped idol? in the endearing of Christ to your soul? in the closer conformity of your mind to God's image? in the purification of your heart? in your more thorough fitness for heaven? Will it not be a real good if it terminate in a revival of God's work within you—in stirring you up to more prayer? in enlarging your heart to all that love the same Savior? in stimulating you to increased activity for the conversion of sinners, for the diffusion of the truth, and for the glory of God?

Oh yes! good, real good, permanent good must result from all the Divine dispensations in your history. Bitter repentance shall end in the experienced sweetness of Christ's love. The festering wound shall but elicit the healing balm. The overpowering burden shall but bring you to the tranquil rest. The storm shall but quicken your footsteps to the Hiding Place. The bitter-cold north wind and the balmy south wind shall breathe together over your garden, and the spices shall flow out.

In a little while—oh, how soon! you shall pass away from earth to heaven, and in its clearer, serener light shall read the truth, often read with tears before, "And we know that all things work together for good to them that love God, to them who are the called according to his purpose."

THE LITTLE THINGS OF LIFE!

"But even the very hairs of your head are all numbered." Luke 12:7

You know so little of God, my reader, because you live at such a distance from God. You have so little communion with Him—so little confession of sin—so little searching of your own conscience—so little probing of your own heart—so little transaction with Him in the little things of life. You deal with God in great matters. You take great trials to God, great perplexities, great needs; but in the minutiae of each day's history, in what are called the little things of life, you have no dealings with God whatever—and consequently you know so little of the love, so little of the wisdom, so little of the glory, of your resplendent covenant God and reconciled Father.

I tell you, the man who lives with God in little matters—who walks with God in the minutiae of his life— is the man who becomes the best acquainted with God— with His character, His faithfulness, His love. To meet God in my daily trials, to take to Him the trials of my calling, the trials of my church, the trials of my family, the trials of my own heart; to take to Him that which brings the shadow upon my brow, that rends the sigh from my heart—to remember it is not too trivial to take to God—above all, to take to Him the least taint upon the conscience, the slightest pressure of sin upon the heart, the softest conviction of departure from God—to take it to Him, and confess it at the foot of the cross, with the hand of faith upon the bleeding sacrifice—oh! these are the paths in which a man becomes intimately and closely acquainted with God!

ALL DROPPING FROM THE OUTSTRETCHED, MUNIFICENT HAND OF A LOVING, GRACIOUS, AND BOUNTIFUL FATHER!

Beloved, remember that all our past and all our coming prosperity, if indeed He shall so appoint it—is in the hand of God. It is His wisdom that suggests our plans, it is His power that guides, and it is His goodness that makes them successful. Every flower that blooms in our path—every smile that gladdens it—every mercy that bedews it, comes to us from our heavenly Father. Oh! for grace to recognize God in all our mercies! How much sweeter will be our sweets—how much more blessed our blessings—and endeared our endearments—to see them all dropping from the outstretched, munificent hand of a loving, gracious, and bountiful Father! Oh! for a heart lifted up in holy returns of love, gratitude and praise!

ALL THE VARIED DEALINGS

"He has done all things well." Mark 7:37

Yes, from first to last—from our cradle to our grave—
from the earliest pang of sin's conviction to the last thrill of
sin's forgiveness—from earth to heaven—this will be our
testimony in all the way the Lord our God has led us in the
wilderness—He has done all things well. In providence and
in grace—in every truth of His Word—in every lesson of
His love—in every stroke of His rod—in every sunbeam
that has shone—in every cloud that has shaded—in every
element that has sweetened—in every ingredient that has
embittered—in all that has been mysterious, inscrutable,
painful, and humiliating—in all that He gave—in all that
He took away—this testimony is His just due, and this our
grateful acknowledgment through time and through
eternity—He has done all things well.

Has He converted us through grace by a way we had
thought the most improbable? Has He torn up all our
earthly hopes by the roots? Has He thwarted our schemes,
frustrated our plans, disappointed our expectations? Has He
taught us in the most difficult schools, by a most severe
discipline, and lessons most humbling to our nature? Has
He withered our strength by sickness? reduced us to
poverty by loss? crushed our heart by bereavement? And
have we been tempted to exclaim, "All these things are
against me?"

Ah! no! faith will yet obtain the ascendancy, and
sweetly sing—"I know in all things that befell, My Jesus
has done all things well." Beloved, it must be so, for Jesus
can do nothing wrong. Study the way of His providence

and grace with the microscopic eye of faith—view them in every light, examine them in their minutest detail, as you would the petal of a flower, or the wing of an insect—and, oh, what wonders, what beauty, what marvelous adaptation would you observe in all the varied dealings with you of your glorious Lord. He has done all things well.

THAT MOST EXCELLENT AND SUPERLATIVE KNOWLEDGE!

There is everything we need in Jesus to endear His name to our hearts. He is our Prophet, teaching us the will of the Father. He is our Priest, offering up Himself as our atoning Victim. He is our King, erecting His throne in our hearts, and subduing us to Himself as His loving and obedient subjects. He is our Friend, loving us at all times. He is our Brother, bone of our bone, and flesh of our flesh, born for our adversity. He is our Great High Priest, touched with the feeling of our infirmities, tempted in all points as we are—and in our sorrows, griefs, and trials encircling us with the many-folded robe of His tender, loving sympathy.

O to know Jesus—that most excellent and superlative knowledge! With Paul we may well count all things but loss for its possession. To know Him as the Savior—to know Him as our Friend—to know Him as our Brother—to know Him as our Advocate—to know Him as our Portion, is endless life and glory!

A SOUL-SATISFYING SPECTACLE!

The sight of Jesus is a soul-satisfying spectacle! The penitent soul is satisfied, for it sees in Jesus a free pardon of sin. The condemned soul is satisfied, for it receives in Jesus a free justification. The believing soul is satisfied, for it discovers in Jesus a fountain of all grace. The tried, tempted, sorrowful soul is satisfied, for it experiences in Jesus all consolation, sympathy and love. Oh, what an all-satisfying Portion is Jesus! He satisfies every holy desire—for He realizes it. He satisfies every craving need—for He supplies it. He satisfies every sore grief—for He soothes it. He satisfies the deepest yearnings, the highest aspirations, the most sublime hopes of the renewed soul—for all these center and end in Him!

THE ALTOGETHER LOVELY ONE!

With what pen, dipped though it were in heaven's brightest hues, can we portray the image of Jesus? The perfection of our Lord was the perfection of holiness. His Deity, essential holiness; His humanity without sin, the impersonation of holiness. All that He was, said, and did, was as flashes of holiness emanating from the fountain of essential purity, and kindling their dazzling and undying radiance around each step He trod. How humble, too, His character! How holy the thoughts He breathed, how pure the words He spoke, how gentle the spirit He exemplified, how tender and sympathizing the outgoings of His compassion and love to man. He is the chief among ten thousand, the altogether lovely one!

THE CHIEF OBJECT OF YOUR STUDY

We know so much of divine truth, my reader, as we have in a measure a personal experience of it in our souls. The mere speculatist and notionalist in religion is as unsatisfactory and unprofitable as the mere theorist and declaimer in science. For all practical purposes both are but ciphers. The character and the degree of our spiritual knowledge begins and terminates in our knowledge of Christ. Christ is the test of its reality—the measure of its depth—and the source of its growth.

If you are advancing in an experimental, sanctifying acquaintance with the Lord Jesus, you are advancing in that knowledge which Paul thus estimates, "I count all things but loss for the excellency of the knowledge of Christ Jesus my Lord." Dear reader, let the chief object of your study be to know the Lord Jesus. It may be in the region of your sinfulness, emptiness, weakness, and foolishness that you learn Him. Nevertheless, however humiliating the school, slow the progress, and limited the attainment, count every fresh step you make in a personal acquaintance with the Lord Jesus as a nobler triumph, and as bringing you into the possession of more real wealth than were the whole chests of human knowledge and science mastered, and its untold treasures poured at your feet.

When adversity comes—when death approaches—when eternity unveils—oh! how indescribably valuable, how inconceivably precious will then be one faith's touch, one faith's glimpse of a crucified and risen Savior! All other attainments then vanish, and the only knowledge that abides, soothes, and comforts, is a heartfelt acquaintance with the most sublime fact of the Gospel—that Jesus came into the world to save sinners. Oh! Whatever other studies may engage your thoughts, do not forget, as you value your eternal destiny, to study the Lord Jesus Christ!

THE MOST ACCESSIBLE AND PRECIOUS SPOT

"Now there stood by the cross of Jesus his mother."
John 19:25

Take your place with Mary, by the cross of Jesus. There meet and blend suffering and love—sorrow and sympathy. Standing in faith by the cross, you are near the suffering Savior, the loving Son, the sympathizing Brother born for your present grief. Jesus, in the depth and tenderness of His love, is at this moment all that He was when, in soul travail, He cast that ineffable look of filial love and sympathy upon His anguished mother.

Likewise, He can enter into your circumstances, understand your grief, sustain and soothe your spirit as one only can, who has partaken of the cup of woe which now trembles in your hand. Drink that cup submissive to His will—for He drank deeply of it before you—and has left the fragrance of His sympathy upon its brim. Your sorrow is not new to Christ. Stand close to the cross of Jesus! It is the most accessible and precious spot this side of heaven— the most solemn and awesome one this side of eternity!

The cross of Jesus is the focus of divine love, sympathy, and power. Stand by it in suffering, in persecution, in temptation. Stand by it in the brightness of prosperity and in the gloom of adversity. Go to Christ's cross in trouble, repair to it in weakness, cling to it in danger, hide beneath it when the wintry storm rushes fiercely over you. Near to the cross, you are near a Father's heart, a Savior's side. You seem to enter the gate of heaven—to stand beneath the vestibule of glory.

Nothing but love will welcome your approach to the cross of Jesus—love that pardons all your sins—flows over all your unworthiness—heals all your wounds—soothes all your sorrows—and will shelter you within its blessed pavilion until earth is changed for heaven, and you lay down the warrior's sword for the victor's palm, and spring from the foot of the cross to the foot of the throne, forever with the Lord!

HOW EMPTYING, HUMBLING, AND ABASING!

Cultivate frequent and devout contemplations of the glory of Christ. Immense will be the benefit accruing to your soul. The mind thus preoccupied, filled, and expanded, will be enabled to present a stronger resistance to the ever advancing and insidious encroachments of the world. No place will be found for vain thoughts, and no desire or time for carnal enjoyments. Oh, how crucifying and sanctifying are clear views of the glory of Emmanuel! How emptying, humbling, and abasing! With the patriarch, we then exclaim, "I abhor myself, and repent in dust and ashes." And with the prophet, "Woe is me! for I am undone; because I am a man of unclean lips, for mine eyes have seen the King, the Lord of hosts." And with the apostle, "But God forbid that I should glory, save in the cross of our Lord Jesus Christ, by whom the world is crucified unto me, and I unto the world."

Oh, then, aim to get your mind filled with enlarged and yet expanding views of the glory of the Redeemer. Let it, in all the discoveries it affords of the Divine mind and majesty, be the one subject of your thoughts—the one theme of your conversation. Place no limit to your knowledge of Christ. Ever consider that you have but read the preface to the volume; you have but touched the fringe of the sea. Stretching far away beyond you, are undiscovered beauties, and precious views, and sparkling glories, each encouraging your advance, inviting your research, and asking the homage of your faith, the tribute of your love, and the dedication of your life.

Go forward, then! The glories that yet must be revealed to you in a growing knowledge of Jesus, what imagination can conceive, what pen can describe them? Jesus stands ready to unveil all the beauties of His person; and to admit you into the very pavilion of His love. There is not a chamber of His heart that He will not throw open to you—not a blessing that He will not bestow upon you—not a glory that He will not show to you.

You shall see greater things than you have yet seen— greater depths of sin in your fallen nature shall be revealed—deeper sense of the cleansing efficacy of the atoning blood shall be felt—clearer views of your acceptance in the Beloved—greater discoveries of God's love—and greater depths of grace and glory in Jesus shall be enjoyed. Your communion with God shall be closer, and more the fruit of adopting love in your heart. Your feet shall be as hinds' feet, and you shall walk on high places. Your peace shall flow as a river, and your righteousness as the waves of the sea. Sorrow shall wound you less deeply—affliction shall press you less heavily—tribulation shall affect you less keenly—all this, and infinitely more, will result from your deeper knowledge of Jesus.

WHEN HIS BEAUTY IS SEEN

O what a Savior is Jesus Christ! He is the chief among ten thousand! Look at His sinless, yet real humanity—without a single taint, yet sympathizing with us in all our various conditions—our afflictions—our temptations—our infirmities—our griefs. Now that He is in glory, He is still cherishing a brother's heart, bending down His ear to our petitions—ever standing near to catch our sighs—to dry our tears—to provide for our needs—to guide us by His counsel—and afterwards to receive us to glory!

O what a Savior is Jesus Christ! When He is known, all other beings are eclipsed. When His beauty is seen, all other beauty fades. When His love is felt, He becomes supremely enthroned in the affections. To know Him more, becomes the one desire of the renewed mind, and to make Him more known, is the one aim of the Christian life. O what a Savior is Jesus Christ!

YOUR ALMIGHTY FRIEND!

Because Jesus is the Almighty God, His people have an Almighty Burden-Bearer. We are a burdened people. Every believer carries a burden peculiar to himself. What is your burden, O believer? Is it indwelling sin? Is it some natural infirmity of the flesh? Is it a constitutional weakness? Is it some domestic trial? Is it a personal or relative trial? Is it the loss of property? Is it the decay of health? Is it soul anxiety? Is it mental despondency?

Come, oppressed and burdened believer, ready to give up all and sink! Behold Jesus, the Almighty God, omnipotent to transfer your burden to Himself, and give you rest! It is well that you are sensible of the pressure— that you feel your weakness and insufficiency—and that you are brought to the end of all your own power. Now turn to your Almighty Friend, who is the Creator of the ends of the earth—the everlasting God, who does not faint, neither is weary.

Oh, what strength there is in Jesus for the weak, and faint, and drooping of His flock! You are ready to succumb to your foes, and you think the battle of faith is lost. Cheer up! Jesus, your Savior, friend, and brother, is the Almighty God, and will perfect His strength in your weakness. The battle is not yours but His! Jesus sustains our infirmities— bears our burdens—supplies our needs— and encircles us with the shield of His Almightiness! What a Divine spring of consolation and strength to the tired and afflicted saint is the Almightiness of Jesus. Your sorrow is too deep—your affliction too heavy—your difficulty too great for any human to resolve. It distances in its intensity and magnitude the sympathy and the power of man.

Come, you who are tossed with tempest and not comforted. Come, you whose spirit is wounded, whose heart is broken, whose mind is bowed down to the dust. Hide for a little while within Christ's sheltering Almightiness! Jesus is equal to your condition. His strength is almighty! His love is almighty! His grace is almighty! His sympathy is almighty! His arm is almighty! His resources are infinite, fathomless, measureless! And all this Almightiness is on your side, and will bring you through the fire and through the water. Almighty to rescue, He is also your Brother and Friend to sympathize. And while His Divine arm encircles, upholds, and keeps you—His human soul, touched with the feeling of your infirmities, yearns over you with all the deep intensity of its compassionate tenderness.

THE ASTONISHING, THE MARVELOUS LOVE!

The cross of Jesus inspires our love to Him. It would seem impossible to be brought by the Holy Spirit to the foot of the cross, and not feel the inspiration of love. Surely a believing apprehension of the amazing, the unparalleled love of Jesus, bending His look of forgiveness upon us from the cross, will thaw our icy hearts into the warmest glow of affection. Believe that Jesus loves you, and your heart shall glow with a love in return which will bear it on in a willing obedience and unreserved surrender, in faithful service and patient suffering, enwrapped, consumed amid the flames of its own heaven inspired and heaven ascending affection. The astonishing, the marvelous love, He has exhibited in giving you His beloved Son to die in your stead, are cords by which He would draw your loving heart to Himself.

BECAUSE HE LOVED HER!

Jesus sustains no association to His Church more expressive than that of the marriage relationship. From all eternity He forever betrothed her to Himself. He asked her at the hands of her Father—and the Father gave her to Him. He entered into a covenant that she would be His. The conditions of that covenant were great, but not too great for His love to undertake. They were, that He should assume her nature, discharge her legal obligations, endure her punishment, repair her ruin, and bring her to glory! He undertook all, and He accomplished all, because He loved her! The love of Jesus to His Church is the love of the most tender husband. It is single, constant, affectionate, matchless, wonderful. Jesus sympathizes with her, nourishes her, provides for her, clothes her, watches over, and indulges her with the most intimate and endearing tenderness.

ETERNALLY REPOSE YOUR WEARY SOUL
IN THE BOSOM OF JESUS

Forward, believer in Christ, to the toils, duties, and trials of another stage of life's journey! Jesus is enough for them all. Jesus will be with you in them all. Jesus will triumphantly conduct you through them all. Beloved one, live in the constant expectation of soon seeing Jesus face to face—conversing with He whom here below, cheered, comforted, and sweetened many a weary step of your Christian pilgrimage. That moment is speeding on. In a little while and all that now wounds and ruffles, tempts and pollutes, will have disappeared like the foam upon the billow, and you shall eternally repose your weary soul in the bosom of Jesus!

THE SOLITARY OBJECT OF HIS LOVE!

It is a great mercy when we can retire from the crowd and deal with God individually—when we can take the precious promises to ourselves individually—when we can repair to Jesus with individual sins, infirmities, and sorrows—feeling that His eye bends its glance upon us—His ear bows down to us—His hand is outstretched to us—His whole heart absorbed in us as though not another petitioner or sufferer offered a request, or unveiled a sorrow. As if, in a word, we were the solitary object of His love!

His invitation to you is, "Come unto Me." He would have you come. You cannot honor Him more than recognizing His personal relation to yourself, and disclosing your personal circumstances, making personal confession of personal sin, presenting personal needs, and unveiling personal infirmities, backslidings, and sorrows.

CHRIST MUST BE ALL!

We cannot keep our eye too exclusively or too intently fixed on Jesus. All salvation is in Him. All salvation proceeds from Him. All salvation leads to Him. And for the assurance and comfort of our salvation we are to repose believingly and entirely on Him. Christ must be all! Christ the beginning—Christ the center—and Christ the end.

Oh sweet truth to you who are sensible of your poverty, vileness, and insufficiency, and of the ten thousand flaws and failures of which, perhaps, no one is cognizant but God and your own soul! Oh, to turn and rest in Christ—a full Christ—a loving Christ—a tender Christ, whose heart's love never chills, from whose eye darts no reproof, from whose lips breathes no sentence of condemnation! Christ must be all!

THAT FRIEND!

"There is a friend that sticks closer than a brother."
Proverbs 18:24

The power of human sympathy is amazing, if it leads the heart to Christ. It is paralyzed, if it leads only to ourselves. Oh, how feeble and inadequate are we to administer to a diseased mind, to heal a broken heart, to strengthen the feeble hand, and to confirm the trembling knees! Our mute sympathy, our prayerful silence, is often the best exponent of our affection, and the most effectual expression of our aid.

But if, taking the object of our solicitude by the hand, we gently lead him to God—if we conduct him to Jesus, portraying to his view the depth of His love, the perfection of His atoning work, the sufficiency of His grace, His readiness to pardon, His power to save, the exquisite sensibility of His nature, and thus His perfect sympathy with every human sorrow—we have then most truly and most effectually soothed the sorrow, healed the wound, and strengthened the hand in God.

There is no sympathy, no love, no gentleness, no tenderness, no patience, like Christ's! Oh how sweet, how encouraging, to know that Jesus sympathetically enters into my afflictions—my temptations—my sorrows—my joys. May this truth endear Him to our souls! May it constrain us to unveil our whole heart to Him, in the fullest confidence of the closest, most sacred, and precious friendship. May it urge us to do those things always which are most pleasing in His sight.

Beloved, never forget—let these words linger upon your ear, as the echoes of music that never die—in all your sorrows, in all your trials, in all your needs, in all your assaults, in all your conscious wanderings, in life, in death, and at the day of judgment—you possess a friend that sticks closer than a brother! That friend is Jesus!

AS THOUGH IT HAD NEVER BEEN!

Beloved, soon, O how soon! all that now loads the heart with care, and wrings it with sorrow—all that dims the eye with tears, and renders the day anxious and the night sleepless, will be as though it had never been! Emerging from the entanglement, the dreariness, the solitude, the loneliness, and the temptations of the wilderness, you shall enter upon your everlasting rest, your unfading inheritance, where there is no sorrow, no declension, no sin, no sunset, no twilight, no evening shadows, no midnight darkness—but all is one perfect, cloudless, eternal day, for Jesus is the joy, the light, and the glory thereof!

WHAT IS HEAVEN?

Beloved, what is heaven? What is the final glory of the saints? Is it not the best place, the richest inheritance provided by the Father for the people ransomed and brought home to glory by His Son? Heaven is a place designated by God, chosen and consecrated by Him for the Church redeemed by the precious blood of His dear Son. And when we enter there, we shall enter as children welcomed to a Father's home! It will be the best that God can give us! He will bestow upon us, who deserved the least, the best in His power to bestow—the best Savior, the best robe, the best banquet, the best inheritance.

In the new heaven and the new earth there will be nothing more to taint, nothing more to sully, nothing more to embitter, nothing more to wound—no serpent to beguile, no Eve to ensnare, no spoiler to destroy, no sin to defile, no adversity to sadden, no misunderstanding to alienate, no tongue to defame, no suspicion to chill, no tear, nor sickness, nor death, nor parting. It will be the best part of the pure, radiant, glorified universe which God will assign to His people! Saints of the Most High!

Let the prospect cheer, sanctify, and comfort you! It will not be long that you are to labor and battle here on earth. It is but a little while that you are to occupy your present sphere of conflict, of trial, and of sorrow. The time is coming—oh, how fast it speeds! Soon the Lord Jesus Christ will bring you home to heaven!

Printed in Poland
by Amazon Fulfillment
Poland Sp. z o.o., Wrocław

74348195R00038